The FACT ATTACK series

Awesome Aliens

Beastly Bodies

Cool Cars

Crazy Creatures

Crucial Cricket

Dastardly Deeds

Deadly Deep

Devastating Dinosaurs

Dreadful Disasters

Fantastic Football

Gruesome Ghosts

Incredible Inventions

Mad Medicine

Magnificent Monarchs

Nutty Numbers

Remarkable Rescues

Rowdy Rugby

Spectacular Space

Super Spies

Vile Vampires

FACT ATTACK

DREADFUL DISASTERS

IAN LOCKE

MACMILLAN CHILDREN'S BOOKS

First published 1998 by Macmillan Children's Books

This edition published 2012 by Macmillan Children's Books
a division of Macmillan Publishers Limited
20 New Wharf Road, London N1 9RR
Basingstoke and Oxford
Associated companies throughout the world
www.panmacmillan.com

ISBN 978-1-4472-2425-9

1 3 5 7 9 8 6 4 2

A CIP catalogue record for this book is available from
the British Library.

Printed and bound by CPI Group (UK) Ltd, Croydon CR0 4YY

DID YOU KNOW THAT . . .

 In 1996 a new supermarket in County Durham was opened and it was discovered that the checkouts were 6 inches too narrow for the trolleys.

 Not long before World War Two broke out, the British government allowed Germany to invade Czechoslovakia. The British prime minister, Neville Chamberlain, called the matter "a quarrel in a faraway country of which we know nothing".

During the seventeenth century a fort was built on an island off the Scilly Isles. It had a series of cannons put on the battlements – but it was found that none of the cannons was able to shoot far enough to hit any ships out at sea!

 In 1993 the ninth commonest cause of injury at work in Britain was animals!

 T.E. Lawrence, who became famous as Lawrence of Arabia during the First World War, wrote his story in the book *Seven Pillars of Wisdom*. He had to write a lot of it twice – he left the first copy of the manuscript on a train in Reading and it was never found.

The American pilot Charles Lindbergh made history when he completed the first solo flight across the Atlantic ocean, from America to Paris, in 1927 in 33 1/2 hours in the *Spirit of St Louis*. He was known as "Lucky Lindy", but his trip was not as easy as it could have been. He had an extra fuel tank put on the front of the plane and as a result had to use a periscope to see where he was going.

Every now and then a famous person is said to be dead when they are very much alive.This happened to:

I. Lord Baden Powell
The founder of the Boy Scouts was said to have been shot as a spy during the First World War. The news was widely reported in the USA.

2. Daniel Boone
The famous frontiersman of US history was reported dead in 1818. Boone

laughed when he read the report. He
died two years later aged 86.

3. Wild Bill Hickock
A legend in his lifetime, this sheriff and
marshal of the "Wild West" read of his
death in a paper in March 1872. He
wrote to the editor to say he was very
much alive.

4. Alfred Nobel
The inventor of dynamite and the
founder of the Nobel prizes was reported
dead by a French paper in 1888. His
obituary sounded so bad that he founded
the Nobel prizes as a result.

5. Mark Twain
After the family of this famous US author
died in 1897, he went into retreat. A
US newspaper then reported he had
died penniless in London. Someone
was sent to confirm the news. Twain
replied: "Reports of my death are greatly
exaggerated."

6. Bertrand Russell

This great English mathematician was reported dead in 1937. The report was reprinted when he actually died in 1970.

7. Robert Graves

The English poet and writer Robert Graves was reported dead during the First World War. He actually died when aged over 90.

8. Paul McCartney

The co-writer of many of the Beatles hits was reported dead by a US college magazine in the late 1960s. The rumour was believed in many places and the present Sir Paul McCartney was said to be an imposter.

9. Eddie Rickenbacker

Eddie Rickenbacker was a famous US air and motor racing ace. In 1942 his plane went missing and he was reported dead. The next month he and his companion were found to have survived

on a raft in the Pacific for 23 days.

10. J.P. Narayan
Reports in 1979 that this leading Indian
politician was dead reached the Prime
Minister, who went to speak over his
"body". Narayan soon recovered.

 America witnessed one of the worst
moments in space history on 27
January 1967. Astronauts Virgil
Grissom, Edward White and Roger
Chaffee entered their Apollo 1 capsule
for a test. In the capsule they were
breathing pure oxygen. A small spark
started a fire in the enclosed space
soon after the astronauts were locked
in. The oxygen turned the fire into a
fireball. Within minutes the men were
dead. The heat of the fire was so great
that it took two hours for the craft to
cool and the bodies to be recovered.

The European Union decided, not long ago, that it would be a good idea to provide the disabled, including the partially sighted and the blind, with a guide to their rights. However, it was only available in print – not on video or in Braille!

 Beekeepers in Brazil were looking for a better type of bee in the 1950s. By 1957 they had a new type of bee which produced more honey. The only problem was that they were killers. Swarms of these bees killed a number of people in Brazil and then moved north as far as America where more people died from their stings.

Larry Yung, a businessman, thought he had made a terrible mistake when he accidentally mixed up his bets at Sha Tin racecourse in Hong Kong in 1992. As it happened, Larry was in luck – he won $5 million!

One of the biggest railway disasters in Britain happened on the night of 28 December 1879. During a storm the North British mail train was about to cross the Tay Bridge (then the longest in the world) when the bridge collapsed, taking the steam train and its carriages with it. All 75 passengers and the crew of five aboard were drowned as the train fell 30 metres into the river. The train itself was found in the river months later with little damage.

Some 700 years ago an English baron, Fitzwaine Fulk, died of suffocation in his armour when his horse got stuck in a bog.

During the 19th century a play called *The Sign of the Cross* was a great success in Britain and America. When the tour of the play began in Britain a live lamb was used as a prop. Problems began when, after weeks of success, the lamb grew into a sheep. In the end the actress carrying the "lamb" collapsed on stage under the weight of the fully grown sheep!

One of the strangest disasters took place at a factory in Boston, USA. The company made black treacle. An explosion emptied a 15-metre tank of the stuff. 20 people were killed and 40 injured after a 5-metre wave of treacle ran through part of the city. It swamped homes and buried a fire station.

Shooting accidents are common in the USA. Harold Erickson was not a good shot. While practising a quick draw in Newhall, California, he managed to shoot himself in both legs.

Some time ago in Leeds, a gang of thieves rented an empty shop next to a bank. They began to dig a tunnel below the shop into the bank. By the time they had completed the job the bank had closed for refurbishment and was empty of cash and other valuables.

Edmund D. Looney of the USA asked a court if he could change his name – he wanted to be a psychiatrist!

 When British Telecom ran an expensive ad campaign for the change of British telephone dialling codes to 01 they used photographs of famous days in history. One of the best known pictures was the first landing on the Moon. The only problem was – they got the date wrong!

 During the BBC's 1987 coverage of the general election, frontman David Dimbleby was seen on camera eating a Mars bar. He later called Mrs Thatcher "Mrs Finchley".

A tornado's speed can reach an incredible 261 mph – the most violent winds known on the surface of the Earth.

When the fossil of the iguanodon dinosaur was first put on show, no one was really sure how the bones should fit together. As a result it ended up on all fours and had one thumb stuck on its head because it was thought to be a horn!

Maybe you can't be lucky all the time. £11 million UK lottery winner Karl Crompton managed to crash two new motorbikes, have one vandalized, spin a Porsche car, break a leg and dislocate a shoulder – all within a year of his win!

Ronald Reagan, the former film star and US President in the 1980s, was sometimes lost for words. He once called Princess Diana, the Princess of Wales, "Princess David". In another speech, supposed to be about Third World countries, he said "The United States has much to offer the Third World War"!

The first man to be killed in a railway accident was MP William Huskisson. On 15 September 1830 he was at the opening of the Liverpool and Manchester railway and was wandering near the *Northumbria* train. Huskisson crossed the track to speak to the Duke of Wellington just as Stephenson's *Rocket* was coming down it. While others nearby got out of the way, Huskisson tripped and fell beneath the wheels of the oncoming train. Though taken by the *Northumbria* to an Eccles hospital he died later that day.

A Spanish air force jet once shot itself down after its gunfire glanced off a mountainside and came back and hit it.

The inventor of the top hat, James Heatherington, was arrested on 5 January 1797 for wearing his new invention in public in London. The hat attracted such a big crowd that several women fainted and a small boy had his arm broken in the crush. Mr Heatherington was told in court that his hat was likely to frighten people and he was fined what was then the huge sum of £50!

Ten well-known stories which include disasters or accidents:

1. *Robinson Crusoe*
The story by Daniel Defoe in which Crusoe is shipwrecked on a desert island. It was based on the true story of the shipwreck of Alexander Selkirk.

2. *Gone with the Wind*
This epic book about the American civil war by Margaret Mitchell includes the disaster of the burning of the city of Atlanta, Georgia.

3. *Gulliver's Travels*
During his adventures, Gulliver is shipwrecked on the island of Lilliput.

4. *Typhoon*
A story by the Polish writer Joseph Conrad which describes the events in a typhoon (a type of hurricane) at sea.

5. *Bleak House*
In this Dickens novel, one of the characters,

Krook, becomes a victim of spontaneous combustion, when he burns for no reason.

6. *Jane Eyre*
Charlotte Brontë's story includes the burning down of Thornfield Hall.

7. *A Shocking Accident*
This story by Graham Greene tells of the accidental death caused by a pig falling on the father of the character Jerome, while he is in Hong Kong.

8. *Lord of the Flies*
The famous story by William Golding about small boys who are left on an island after an air crash.

9. *The Last Days of Pompeii*
This story, by Bulwer Lytton, tells of the eruption of Mount Vesuvius in AD 79.

10. *The Lost World*
The famous story of a prehistoric world by Sir Arthur Conan Doyle (used by Spielberg

in his film) in which the team of Professor Challenger have to flee an erupting volcano, keeping only dinosaur eggs to prove they had found the lost world.

The first deaths in road accidents in Britain were recorded as long ago as 1873.

A record 324 twisters (or tornadoes) struck the USA in May 1957.

Among the best-known writers in Victorian times was Thomas Carlyle. He sent his only copy of his *History of the French Revolution* to his friend John Stuart Mill to look at. Mill's maid thought the manuscript was waste paper and burned it.

The man who founded the Bank of England was called John Patterson. He became convinced that a place called the Yucatan peninsula, near Mexico, was heaven on Earth, and he managed to persuade a large number of Scottish people to go there. The whole trip was a disaster, many of the Scots lost their lives through disease and starvation and the cost was so great that it was one of the reasons why the Scots agreed to unite with England.

A woman in Romania was being carried to her funeral when she woke up, jumped out of the coffin and ran off along the road. Unfortunately she ran straight into the path of an oncoming car and was knocked down and killed!

Nine strange events as a result of hurricanes and tornadoes:

1. Clouds of tarantula spiders have been blown in by hurricanes in the USA.

2. In one hurricane in the USA birds sitting on a branch had all their feathers blown off!

3. In Iowa in 1962 a cow flew nearly a kilometre (half a mile) after being sucked up in a tornado.

4. A baby was once whisked up into a hurricane. He was found some way away,

perfectly well, almost without a scratch.

5. After the Great Tempest in Britain in 1703 a cow was found alive after being blown into the top branches of a tree.

6. A British man slept through almost all the 1987 hurricane, until a tree crashed through his roof into his bedroom!

7. During Hurricane Inez in 1966, stranded people became so hungry that they opened cans of food with their teeth.

8. After a hurricane in Indianola in Texas in 1886 the town was abandoned.

9. A five-minute tornado in St Louis in the USA in late September 1927 killed 69 and injured 600!

The British Parliament looked at Edison's invention of the electric light. They believed it would have no use and would be of no interest to "practical or scientific men".

 During the night of 15 October 1987 a great storm with hurricane winds hit Britain. It caused £1,000 million of damage, the highest figure ever recorded for weather damage in Britain's history. Before it hit, a woman rang the main weather forecast station and said she had heard there was a hurricane on the way. That evening, on the BBC TV weather news, the weatherman told the woman not to worry, there was no hurricane in sight! In Shoeburyness, Essex, the wind was the strongest recorded there for 500 years.

An eccentric Englishman in the eighteenth century once set fire to his nightshirt to try and cure his hiccups. It is not known if he survived the cure.

 One of the passengers on the first railway service, covering four miles from Swansea to Oystermouth in 1807, felt so dizzy after the journey, at 16 miles an hour, he thought it would take him a week to recover!

John Farynor was a royal baker in London during the time of Charles II. One night in 1666 he went to bed, forgetting to put out the fire in his bread ovens. At two in the morning, on Sunday 2 September 1666, the fire sent out sparks to a pile of hay in the building next door. The Great Fire of London had begun. House after house in the narrow London streets caught fire. The Mayor was told, but thought nothing of it, as such fires were quite common among the wooden houses. So it was not until that afternoon that the scale of the fire became obvious, as the warehouses along the river Thames caught fire. By Wednesday 13,000 houses had been burned, 57 churches were destroyed and shops were ruined. At St Paul's Cathedral the fire was so hot the ancient tombstones cracked and turned to dust, the metal decorations melted and the lead from the roof ran in rivers. The fire was only stopped from spreading by teams who knocked down buildings in its path. Though a disaster, the fire did have some good effects – the old slums of

London were cleared and the plague was at last wiped out.

A woman once stayed in bed for 40 years – only because her doctor forgot to come back to see her. When she first went to bed, her doctor had said she had flu and was not to get up until he returned. He never did come back!

In 1912 the *Evening Sun* newspaper in the USA ran a headline: "All saved from *Titanic* after collision". It reported that the ship was still afloat and was being towed to a harbour in Canada. In fact, the *Titanic* disaster was one of the worst events to happen at sea; over 1,300 died. The *Daily Express* in England made the same mistake, saying that all the passengers had been saved.

In 1996 a group of clairvoyants (people who claim to be able to predict the future) turned up in Paris for a conference. They were a week late and had missed it!

At the age of 16, Bette Davis, who went on to be one of the biggest stars in Hollywood, posed nude for a statue of the Goddess Diana. The sculpture is still on show at Boston's Museum of Fine Arts.

Both fullbacks in a Chester football club match on 1 January 1966 broke their legs during the game.

A hairdresser, Leonard Moore, from Kentucky in the USA, decided to try and row across the Bering Straits from Russia to Finland in a bath. His only food seemed to be four gallons of peanut butter. The weather was so cold his peanut butter was frozen solid by the fifth day. The next day Mr Moore gave up his attempt when the water froze around his bath.

In the 400 metres at the Olympics in London in 1908, only one man, Lieutenant Wyndham Halswells of Britain, was left in the final after the other competitors were accused of cheating and withdrew in protest.

After the British set fire to the White House, the President's home in Washington, USA, in 1812, it was only saved from complete destruction because of a thunderstorm which put out the flames.

When 250,000 people demonstrated in Washington, the American capital, for a cleaner environment and the use of solar energy, on Sun Day in the 1970s, they left behind litter over ten acres of ground.

A British man in Skopje, Yugoslavia, had a lucky escape in the 1960s. He tried to book into the two biggest hotels in the city the night before a quake struck. They were full so he went to a third. When he woke in the morning he found that the other two hotels had collapsed in ruins.

The inventor of the first two-wheeled bicycle, a Scotsman, was prosecuted for dangerous driving.

In 1970 the British Royal Navy began practice torpedo firing from a submarine off the Isle of Bute, Scotland. Something went wrong when a torpedo ran through the rough and stopped on the first green of the Kingarth links golf club where some golfers were just beginning their game! The Navy later turned up to collect their missing torpedo.

When US actress and model Brooke Shields married tennis star Andre Agassi in April 1997, the ring used was one that Agassi had bought Brooke some time before. The real wedding ring, worth $60,000, had been accidentally put out with the rubbish! After the wedding, which took place in the church on the Del Monte golf course in California, someone had to be sent out to a skip to find it. The couple are now divorced.

Investigators couldn't understand why fires kept breaking out in a rubber factory in Ohio in the USA. In the end they found that they were started by a woman who was so electric she carried 30,000 volts.

 When the first example of the duck-billed platypus arrived at the British Museum from Australia, the officials thought it was a fake and tried to pull its beak off.

 General Haig, a leader of the British Army in the First World War, did not think machine guns were any good. He refused to accept they would help in battle.

The strongest earthquake to hit Britain happened near Colchester in Essex on 22 April 1884.

Queen Victoria came to the throne aged 18 in 1837. When she was crowned the next year, the Archbishop of Canterbury put the coronation ring on her fourth finger, rather than her little finger, for which it was made. It caused her a lot of pain when she tried to take it off. An 88-year-old peer, Lord Rolle, tripped and rolled down the steps as he was paying homage to the new queen. A little later it was found that part of the ceremony had been missed and everyone was called back to complete the coronation. The Queen's first job after arriving back at Buckingham Palace was to give her dog a bath.

Gold was first discovered in Australia in 1823, but the government were frightened about what might happen in a gold rush so news of the find was banned.

Acid in the air produced by the burning of fossil fuels leads to acid rain. Acid rain has not only destroyed forests and woodland, it also dissolved the gold roof of Cracow cathedral in Poland.

In 1977, US officials admitted that a tree planted by President Carter in Washington, County Durham, was dead. The town was where the family of the first American president, George Washington, came from. The tree had been frozen to death on its flight from the USA. The President finished the planting with twelve spades of earth and one for luck – he knew it was dead.

The US actress Tallulah Bankhead once
turned up in May 1920 to see a friend
at a theatre in New York. Her friend
was surprised to see her, telling her,
"It's only three thirty – why aren't you at
your play?" Tallulah Bankhead suddenly
realized she had walked off the stage
after the first act of the play in which she
was appearing, thinking it was over.

In 1977 the Doncaster rugby league side
set a record for losing forty games on the
trot. In muddy conditions they were unable
to recognize their own jerseys and often
tackled each other.

President Johnson of America was
once taken to see troops at a US
base, being told they were on their
way to Vietnam. In fact they had just
come back. The President insisted on
watching them take off again.

Only one person has been killed by an earthquake in Britain – an apprentice killed in London by a falling stone during a quake in 1580.

While installing a computer for a company, two workers used the computer to heat their pies. After two hours they found that the pies had fallen into a part of the computer they could not reach. It took them three hours to get them out and the next day they had to explain the missing three hours in their schedule.

Eighteen publishers turned down a small book called *Jonathan Livingstone Seagull* by Richard Bach in 1970. When it was published it sold 7 million copies in the US alone in five years! The paperback rights were sold for a record $1 million.

When films were first shown, no one knew what effect they might have on those who saw them. Some people panicked when they first saw "moving pictures", thinking the scene was real. A Dublin doctor took films very seriously. He said that people going to films should wear dark glasses and not watch the screen for more than a minute at a time in case they were blinded.

Peter Harvey could have been a player in the record-breaking All Blacks rugby team which toured Britain in 1905. However, the prime minister of New Zealand said he could not go because he was the only qualified lip-reader in the country!

A boy riding in a van in Maryport, Cumberland, decided to throw an unwanted Mars bar out of the window. It hit a professional wrestler and knocked him unconscious. The boy was later fined £10.

After an earthquake off Japan a tsunami (or tidal wave) at a record height of 28 metres was recorded.

How to turn disaster into triumph. Lasse Viren of Finland tripped and fell during the final of the 10,000 metres at the 1972 Olympics. Though he lost about five seconds, he decided to get up and continue the race. By the next lap he had caught up with the main field and he went on to win in a world record time of 27 minutes and 38.4 seconds!

 One in five of all road accidents in Sweden is said to involve a moose.

 A toilet lid lock was invented by an American to stop the use of toilets without permission. It was patent number 3,477,070.

A machine which records earthquakes is called a seismograph. One was kept at the Selfridges store on Oxford Street, London, for many years until it was given to the Science Museum in London.

Gold fever hit the area known as the Klondike in the Yukon in 1896. Charlie Anderson, a Swede, bought Claim 29 for $800 while drunk. When he had sobered up he tried to sell it but no one was interested, so he decided to have a go at digging there himself. In four years he found $1.2 million of gold in his mine. Alec McDonald of Nova Scotia did even better. He gave a hungry Russian prospector a sack of flour in exchange for Claim 30. He later walked away with an incredible $20 million. The chances of striking it lucky were slim – at most four people in a hundred in the Yukon actually found gold.

When Charles Darwin, who became famous for his theory of evolution, was a schoolboy, his parents were sent his report. It said the boy cared "for nothing but shooting, dogs and rat-catching and you will be a disgrace to yourself and all your family". Within ten years of the publication of his famous book *On the Origin of Species by Means of Natural Selection* in 1859 he was famous and became an inspiration to scientists around the world.

The Americans thought the US Secretary of State was mad when he bought Alaska from the Russians for two cents an acre or a total of $7.2 million in gold in 1867. Alaska is now one of the world's richest areas.

The then President of the Philippines, Fidel Ramos, turned up late for a meeting on the day National Punctuality week was launched in 1997. He had got up at four in the morning to watch the US golfer Tiger Woods win the US Masters golf tournament, then gone back to bed. He was woken late after he overslept.

In November 1996 it was found that a new footbridge across the River Yeo near Bristol was 40 cm too short because a government agency sent the wrong measurements to the builders.

The entire Tunisian team in the riding part of the Pentathlon at the Olympics in 1960 fell off their horses – it was the first time anyone had scored 0 in an Olympic event. In the shooting part of the event their aim was so wild they were ordered from the field because they were putting lives in danger.

Early in 1979 it was found that the US government had spent $279,000 building a community centre in the middle of nowhere in the state of Michigan. It had no road and the building was only discovered when it fell down.

The great American writer Mark Twain decided against putting $5,000 into a new invention, the telephone, by Alexander Graham Bell. Instead he put $250,000 into another company which went bust.

Things famous people probably wished they had not done:

1. David Bowie once released a single called "The Laughing Gnome".

2. In the 1980s Lord Dacre Trevor-Roper, a well-known British historian, said that the diaries of Nazi leader Adolf Hitler were real. They turned out to be fakes.

3. The American star actor Warren Beatty appeared in *Ishtar*; the movie was one of the biggest flops ever.

4. Prince Charles once admitted he talked to flowers.

5. Sir Winston Churchill refused to appear on television, believing it was of interest to only a small number of people.

6. Lord Ismay, head of the White Star shipping company, declared that the *Titanic* was unsinkable.

When the first Impressionist paintings went on show in Paris in 1874 the critics made fun of the pictures and most of the public thought they were no good.

 In the early nineteenth century an Irish professor, Dr Lardner, said that if trains went at a speed of over 130 miles an hour, the passengers would all be choked to death.

 The Duc of Albuquerque, a Spanish aristocrat, made racing history in 1963 when he had bets of 66-1 against his finishing the Grand National. He entered the race seven times, and fell or went out of the race every time. In 1965 his horse collapsed. In 1974 he even fell off during training, riding in the race itself with a broken collarbone and his leg in plaster.

Some well-known people have died
in strange ways. King Charles VIII of
France was showing Queen Anne of
Brittany on to a tennis court when
he bashed his head on a beam
and died soon afterwards from a
fractured skull.

On 10 December 1903 a leading
US paper, the *New York Times*,
said that any research into
"aeroplanes" was a waste of time
and money. Only a week later the
Wright brothers made the first
successful manned flight at Kitty
Hawk, North Carolina!

The first hydrogen balloon was flown by Frenchman J. A. C. Charles over France in 1783. He climbed to 1,000 metres then came down in a field about 25 km from Paris. There the balloon was attacked by peasants who believed it was an evil spirit or a moon "that had broken loose" and tore it to shreds. The King heard about the adventure and was so impressed that he introduced a law forbidding people to attack any air balloon.

The American inventor Lee De Forest was arrested in 1913 for trying to sell shares in a radio company. The court was told that his ideas were "absurd".

In 1970 a record company in the US released an album, *The Best of Marcel Marceau*. On each side there was 20 minutes of silence followed by 20 minutes of applause. Marcel Marceau was one of the world's most famous mime artists and never spoke on stage. The record sold quite well!

When the great composer Mozart died at the early age of 35 in 1791, his wife wanted him buried as cheaply as possible in Vienna. When the time came for his funeral it was raining, so she decided not to go. As a result his remains were put into a common grave for paupers. When she tried to find it later no one was able to say where he was buried.

British Rail once made a complete mess of their timetable. Not only were they wrong, but the second timetable they issued to correct the first was wrong – as was the third!

 In the early 1800s a British scientist said that trying to light streets by gas was as impossible as using "a slice of the moon" for light.

 Sam Thomas of Yarmouth decided to steal a sheepskin coat from a hotel lobby. Afterwards he thumbed a lift on a coach. To his amazement the coach was filled with forty senior police officers on their way back from Bognor. Two minutes later one of the policemen recognized the stolen sheepskin coat as his own. Mr Thomas was swiftly taken to the nearest police station.

Royal Ascot is one of the biggest horseracing events in Britain, held at the course at Ascot in Berkshire. In 1993 a woman tried to enter the Sovereign's Gate, to go into the Royal Enclosure. The woman was told by Eric Petheridge, "I'm sorry, love, you can't come in here." The person he tried to turn away was Princess Anne. He didn't recognize her.

In 1920 the *New York Times* newspaper printed an article which made fun of the rocket experiments of Dr Goddard. On 17 July 1969, just as man was about to land on the Moon, the paper apologized for its mistake.

In the 1912 University Boat Race, the boats of both Oxford and Cambridge sank.

Sometimes names are very important. For some reason certain names seem right, others not right. The following list shows how this can be true:

1. Robert Louis Stevenson's first name for *Treasure Island* was *The Sea Cook*.

2. Huddersfield rugby league club still play at a ground called Fartown.

3. The first name given to the great English racehorse Desert Orchid was Fred – thankfully someone decided to change it.

4. The Beatles song released under the title *Yesterday* was first called *Scrambled Eggs*.

5. Sherlock Holmes was originally called Sherringford, until author Arthur Conan Doyle changed it.

6. The name of a game invented by Major Walter Wingfield in Britain in 1839 was Sparistike. Someone decided it should have a better name – it is now lawn tennis.

7. When they first appeared, military tanks did not have a name. On being sent to France in World War One, they were delivered in crates which were said to contain water tanks. So they became known as tanks by accident.

8. Arsenal football club was first named Dial Square football club.

9. The band Rain changed its name to Oasis in 1993.

Heavy rain often interrupted the outdoor events at the Montreal Olympics, Canada, in 1976. One day the Olympic torch was put out by the rain – it was relit by a member of the stadium staff using a rolled-up newspaper.

Florence Nightingale decided, after she came back from the Crimean War in 1856, that she had heart disease and would soon die. So she went to bed – she stayed there for 54 years, eventually dying in 1910 aged 90!

When she was born, the future Queen of France Marie Antoinette had such a bad horoscope that celebrations to mark her birthday were cancelled. When she became Queen of France she was known for living in a fantasy world, mostly at the Palace of Versailles. When the French Revolution came in 1789 she was arrested with the King and was eventually guillotined in 1793.

 Berwick-upon-Tweed, the town on the borders of England and Scotland, is special. In official documents, the town is listed separately. So, in 1856, when the Crimean War broke out, Russia was at war with Great Britain, Ireland, the British Dominions and . . . Berwick-upon-Tweed! When the peace treaty ending the war was signed later that year, the document missed off Berwick-upon-Tweed. Only in 1966 did Russia and Berwick-upon-Tweed declare peace.

The Greek mathematician Pythagoras believed that some human souls became beans after death!

When it was built, the great French palace of Versailles, near Paris, had no lavatories or bathrooms.

In 1803 the French Emperor Napoleon sold the Louisiana Territory to the Americans for four cents an acre. It doubled the size of America and is thought to be the most worthwhile purchase of land in history.

During the terrific earthquake in Lisbon in 1755, three quakes hit the city, followed by waves which reached up to 25 metres. Fires broke out in the city and many great works of art were consumed, along with thousands of rare and valuable books. The prison walls collapsed and hundreds of prisoners made their escape. After the earthquake there were 500 aftershocks, which were felt as far away as England and the West Indies.

Le Bateau (the boat), a painting by the great modern French painter Matisse, was shown upside down in the Museum of Modern Art, New York, for almost seven weeks.

The first rabbits, three pairs, were taken to Australia in the nineteenth century. In under ten years the rabbits had turned into an expensive plague – there were millions of them.

In Shakespeare's play *Julius Caesar* there is a line about a clock striking. Clocks did not appear until about a thousand years after Caesar's death.

In Victorian times an expert on diamonds was told that diamond fields had been discovered in South Africa. The man refused to believe it, saying the gems were probably ostrich droppings.

In 1891 James Bartley was swallowed by a whale. He stayed inside the whale's stomach for two days. He survived and lived until 1926.

The ducks used in the film *Doctor Dolittle*, made in 1967, sank when they were put on a pond. They were moulting and had lost their waterproof feathers!

A woman who kept house for the Minister of War was sentenced to two years in jail and fined £500 for covering her pots of jam with bits of top-secret military documents.

 Cyril Gadney, the referee for the Wales v Ireland rugby union international on 14 May 1936, was refused entry to the ground. He was told that lots of people had tried to get in for free by saying they were the referee and he should go and buy a ticket. Just before the game was due to begin Mr Gadney was found in the queue for tickets.

 Worcester cricket club found in 1889 that their pitch had been sown with turnip seed instead of grass seed by mistake.

Andrew Southern, aged 16, a pupil at Elliott Durham Comprehensive in Nottingham, who had a five-year 100% punctuality and attendance rate, was given a VIP trip to his school as a reward. On 10 May 1997, he was collected by a chauffeur-driven limousine from his home for the drive to his school. But the car got stuck in traffic and he was late, by twenty minutes, for the first time in five years!

The worst British accident at sea in recent times happened when the Townsend Thoresen cross-Channel ferry *Herald of Free Enterprise* capsized off Zeebrugge, Belgium, on 6 March 1987. 193 people died in the accident when the bow doors of the ship were left open by mistake and the sea flooded in.

The worst accident in space occurred on 28 January 1986, when US space shuttle Challenger exploded 73 seconds after take-off from Cape Canaveral in Florida. Among those who died was teacher Christa McAuliffe, who was the first ordinary American to go into space. She had been selected from 11,146 who applied for the job.

 900,000 were killed in a flood after the Huang river, China, burst its banks in October 1887.